*With appreciation, gratitude
and our compliments*

Kahler Lodging Hotels . . .

The Kahler Hotel
Kahler Plaza Hotel
Holiday Inn Downtown
Clinic View Inn & Suites

THE GEESE OF SILVER LAKE

Craig Blacklock

VOYAGEUR PRESS

For my parents, Les and Fran

Acknowledgments

Although I have spent many days observing geese, I am by no means an authority on them, and am deeply grateful to the people who have helped to gather information on these birds. In particular, I wish to thank Dr. James Cooper of the University of Minnesota; Dr. Harold C. Hanson of the Illinois Natural History Survey; Art Hawkins, formerly of the U.S. Bureau of Sports, Fisheries and Wildlife; and Jack Heather and Tony Stegan of the Minnesota Department of Natural Resources. These men provided, or led me to, the information needed to write the manuscript, and many of them read parts of it for accuracy.

Differing accounts of the early history of the geese at Silver Lake. Memories and written records regarding events that took place at East Meadows Ranch are not always the same. And there are numerous opinions regarding the taxonomy of Canada geese. In writing the history, I have chosen to use numbers and dates that I came across most frequently. With regards to taxonomy and behavior, I have tried to express the different opinions or accounts.

Finally, I would like to thank my wife, Nadine, for her continual help in editing the manuscript and in the selection and sequencing of photographs.

* * *

Printed in Hong Kong 89 90 91 92 93 5 4 3 2 1

Library of Congress Cataloging-in-Publication Data

Blacklock, Craig.
    The geese of Silver Lake : text and photographs / by Craig Blacklock
      p.   cm.
      Bibliography: p.
      ISBN 0-89658-114-4 : $15.00
      1. Canada goose—Minnesota—Silver Lake (Olmsted County)
2. Canada goose—Minnesota—Silver Lake (Olmsted County)—Pictorial works. 3. Silver Lake (Olmsted County, Minn.)—
History.   I. Title.
QL696.A52B53   1989
598.4′1—dc20
                                                                                                      89-35631
                                                                                                          CIP

Published by Voyageur Press, Inc.
P.O. Box 338
123 North Second Street   In Minn 612-430-2210
Stillwater, MN 55082 U.S.A.   Toll Free 800-888-9653

Voyageur Press books are also available at discounts in bulk quantities for premium or sales-promotion use. For details contact the Marketing Manager. Please write or call for our free catalog of natural history publications.

THE GEESE OF SILVER LAKE

Craig Blacklock

Fog rises from the small tree-lined lake below me. Shooting up from the horizon a yellow column of sunlight reflects off ice crystals. Over twenty thousand giant Canada geese float on the lake or rest along the shore on a ledge of ice. Mixed into the flock are several species of ducks and other races of Canada geese. As the sun clears the horizon, it reveals that the silhouetted birds are almost all resting with their heads turned over their backs, their bills under feathers. They are, for the most part, silent, nearly motionless—conserving energy during the cold of morning. Ice formed around some of the geese that spent the night in shallow water, and a thick layer of frost covers their feathers.

A predator passes by among the trees and makes a rush for some of the geese on shore, causing them to spring up and fly a short distance to open water. Geese that were sealed in by new ice wiggle about until a rim of water appears around them, and rather awkwardly step onto the ice. Those in the water become alert and swim towards the predator, keeping an eye on it until it trots off. The disturbance doesn't last long, and soon many geese return to shore.

The predator wasn't a coyote or wolf; it was a golden retriever out for a morning jog with its owner. The lake is not a remote prairie pothole left by the glaciers, or a quiet backwater of the Mississippi; it isn't even a natural lake. It is a dammed-up stretch of the south branch of the Zumbro River, right in the heart of Rochester, Minnesota, a city of around sixty thousand people and home of the famous Mayo Clinic.

Today the sight of large flocks of giant Canada geese is not uncommon in many areas of the United States and Canada. However, as recently as 1961, most ornithologists erroneously thought the giant Canada goose was extinct.

The giant is the largest of fifteen races of Canada geese currently recognized by the governments of the United States and Canada. These races range from geese the size of a three-pound mallard on up to the giants that commonly weigh as much as fourteen to sixteen pounds.

Canada geese return to the same breeding areas each year, and over time, adaptation to the physical makeup of these breeding areas produced the size and coloration differences that distinguish different races. These physical differences are graduated in a staircase manner. Generally the races get smaller the further north they nest. Although biologists with the expertise recognize the various races, they often refer to the geese as simply large, medium, or small.

Unquestionably, there are many variations of Canada geese with distinct geographic nesting areas; but biologists debate how many clear distinctions can be made regarding races and species. One study nearing completion has accounted for about 125 races belonging to three distinct species.

But lack of consensus over classification is not new. Records of very large Canada geese go back at least to the 1860s; ornithologists, however, were slow to give recognition to the giant birds. Letters describing exceptionally large geese, some in private flocks, were often met with disbelief.

The giant Canada goose wasn't formally described until the publication of a paper by Jean Delacour in 1947, and later in his book *The Waterfowl of the World*. Delacour based his description on some skins and on notes loaned to him by the wife of the late biologist James Moffitt, who had worked for the California Fish and Game Department. In his book, Delacour wrote, "The Giant Canada Goose appears to be extinct." Other writers on the subject were less cautious and used the definite verb "is" in front of "extinct," and the giant's passing became accepted as fact.

Giant Canada geese originally bred over much of the Midwest, the eastern Great Plains, and southern Manitoba. Most likely, wintering geese long ago used the prairies and spring-fed rivers of the Rochester area. But by the 1920s, the free-flying population of Canada geese had seemingly disappeared. The story of their comeback in the Rochester area begins with Dr. Charles H. Mayo, Sr.

Dr. Mayo purchased a farm tucked into the hills near Rochester and continued adding acreage until his holdings amounted to three thousand acres, to be known as Mayowood. One of Dr. Mayo's recreational farming projects was raising Canada geese. He started his flock with at least one pair purchased in the early 1920s from either the Dakotas or Michigan. Probably he bought more from North Dakota, and by 1929 his flock totaled twenty-two. The geese eventually strayed away and dispersed locally, making a home of Mayowood Lake and other areas around

Rochester.

In 1926, a forty-eight-square mile game refuge was established around Rochester, primarily due to the efforts of Louis Wilson, a member of the local Izaak Walton League. Dr. Mayo's escaped geese, and the protection from hunting, apparently attracted wild flocks. In 1939, Dr. Mayo wrote to the National Association of Audubon Societies, "I am very much interested in the preservation of wildlife and on my farm feed between 500 and 600 Canada geese." In the fall of 1943, Matt Saari, a former game warden, estimated that four thousand Canada geese were in the vicinity of Rochester.

Silver Lake, twenty-five acres in size, was formed in 1936 when a WPA project dammed the south branch of the Zumbro River. With the hope of establishing a flock of nesting geese at this new lake in the park, the city purchased and released six geese there. In 1945, the first three goslings were reared, but vandals killed seven birds the following winter. Five geese were purchased to replace the destroyed birds. Another twelve large geese with pinioned wings joined the Silver Lake flock in 1947, having been willed to the city by a former Mayo Clinic patient from Nebraska who had taken pleasure in watching the geese at Silver Lake. Apparently, these nineteen geese decoyed in wild flocks that had been wintering at Mayowood Lake and the river below. Migrant flocks began stopping over in Silver Lake in 1945.

In 1948, the Rochester Public Utilities began operation of a coal-fired power plant. Water used for cooling purposes was returned to Silver Lake fifteen degrees warmer, raising the lake temperature by five degrees, and thus keeping the lake mostly ice-free throughout the winter. That year, five hundred geese were using Silver Lake in February; the flock doubled in size the following winter and continued to increase.

Five hundred miles away, a project was about to begin that would later prove significant to the Silver Lake flock. H. Albert Hochbaum brought eleven geese from the Delta Waterfowl Research Station to the East Meadows Ranch on Marshy Point, in the interlake region of Manitoba. There, he and a Mr. W. A. Murphy started holding a breeding captive flock. They added to the flock, which built up to about sixty-four birds when many of the geese escaped in 1954 after a flood destroyed the pens.

Warm water discharged from a power plant keeps Silver Lake mostly ice free throughout the winter.

The remaining geese were released in 1956.

In January of 1962, Forrest Lee of the Minnesota Department of Conservation, invited Dr. Harold C. Hanson, senior scientist with the Illinois Natural History Survey, to help band, weigh, and measure geese from the Silver Lake flock.

On a cold, windy morning, the two men were joined by Bob Jessen, Tom Hanson, and George Meyers of the Minnesota Department of Conservation, and Harvey Nelson, Art Hawkins, and Bill Ellerbrock of the U.S. Bureau of Sport Fisheries and Wildlife. The men began weighing trapped birds, but stopped when the weights they were getting were far heavier than they felt could be possible. Assuming their scales must be faulty, Art Hawkins purchased five pounds of sugar and ten pounds of flour to check the weights on the scales. Their scales proved to be correct. A number of people had been puzzled by these apparently large birds for some time—the mystery of their identity was about to be solved.

Dr. Hanson returned to Illinois with the weight records and nine skins. He checked these against Delacour's description and found that the Rochester flock was made up primarily of giant Canada geese—a wintering flock of thousands of geese of a race that was supposedly extinct!

Among the birds the men weighed were two that had been raised and banded at East Meadows Ranch. Researchers would later show that Marshy Point was one of the areas in the interlake region the Silver Lake geese were nesting and that it was a major staging ground, or gathering place, for these geese prior to the fall migration.

The Silver Lake flock was not the only population of giant Canada geese that had been previously unidentified or misidentified. Hanson's continuing surveys during 1962 and 1963 found a total of approximately 54,600 Canada geese in the wild and over 7,200 in captive flocks in North America that fitted Delacour's description of "giants."

At about the same time the Silver Lake geese were discovered to be giants, many concerned people realized that as the city of Rochester expanded the refuge was becoming too small. In the spring of 1962, the Minnesota Department of Natural Resources approved expansion of the refuge to 66½ square miles, and Silver Lake continued to attract more geese each winter.

How low the total numbers of giant Canada geese ever fell is hard to know. Certainly Silver Lake, with its open water, protection from hunting, and close proximity to abundant food, played an important role in the resurgence of giant Canada goose numbers. Today it remains one of the most important wintering grounds of this race.

Restoration efforts have been successful not only at Silver Lake. Giant Canada geese have been reestablished throughout their original breeding range in the United States and Canada, and introduced in several other states and provinces.

When ice is present, the geese make use of the extra standing room. Silver Lake is one of the most important wintering grounds for giant Canada geese.

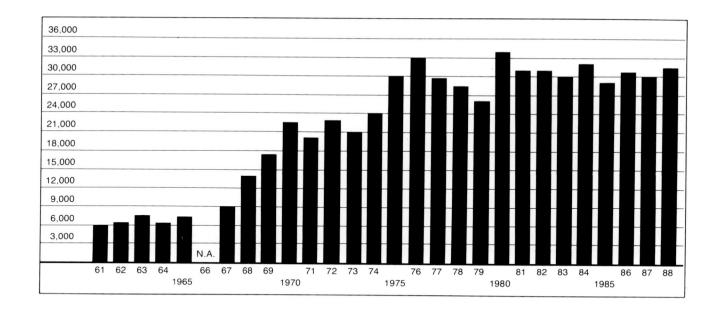

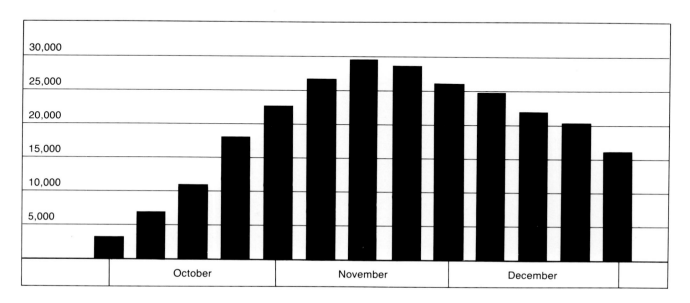

From the time the first skeins of geese arrive from the north in the fall until most of the flock leaves again in the spring, Silver Lake functions as a safe roosting ground. A few hours of observing the geese at Silver Lake reveal that family units are still intact, small flocks within the larger one. The families migrated south together and will remain together throughout most of the winter.

There is a distinct pecking order in the flock that is continually reinforced. The order of dominance generally places the pairs with the largest families on top; beneath them rank pairs without young, single adults, yearlings, and at the bottom, lone immature birds. Interestingly, an immature bird accompanied by a dominant parent may show dominance over a single adult.

Occupying a top position in the hierarchy is a great advantage; it means holding preferred roosting and feeding locations in winter, as well as not having to endure being picked on. Individual geese tend to be found in the same area of Silver Lake day after day. I find this analogous to behavior in my high school cafeteria. Each day hundreds of students entered a room full of nearly identical tables, and yet they usually ended up sitting with the same companions at the same table as the day before. We all knew our standing within a small social circle and could be sure of our acceptance if we sat in the same place. Moving to another table, into the realm of another clique, produced stress and possible conflict.

Occasionally a family group appears to be double the size of the others. This probably results from a crèche that was formed when the young of one or more families got mixed in with the young of another and all were taken over by one pair of adults. This phenomenon most often occurs when the young are less than a week old. Gang broods may also form when the young are several weeks old and families begin establishing loose flocks. The young intermix and may be taken over by the dominant pair. Some people feel this sort of behavior most likely occurs between geese that are related. A large family group may also be composed of three generations.

Such a large family can be very dominant. I watched a gander pushing his way through a sleeping flock, pecking and chasing many birds out of the way. Eighteen geese were in his wake. He then turned to them, stretched out his neck, and opened his bill wide with tongue out, honking wildly in a typical display known as a Triumph Ceremony. All eighteen birds responded in kind, indicating they were all related. The Triumph Ceremony may be seen among siblings from the time they are a week old, and seems to reinforce family ties. Pairs also display this behavior, especially following any form of aggression on the gander's part towards other geese, or following a separation of the pair. It is not unlike hockey players' communal hug following a goal.

This "team spirit" expands to the whole flock whenever danger intrudes. The reaction the geese had to the golden retriever, mentioned earlier, is a typical response to a land-bound threat, and many a predator has been frustrated by a flock of geese following it about just out of reach, their alert attitude announcing its presence to the whole lake. This defense behavior proved the downfall of many geese in the past, as hunters used their dogs to "toll" the geese within range.

Danger can also come from above. On several occasions, noticing a goose with its head tipped sideways looking skyward, I have sighted a mere dot of a hawk circling overhead. Should an eagle, or even a helicopter, fly over, the geese immediately fall silent and swim to the center of the lake where they could dive underwater to safety.

Attacks from beneath the water come from snapping turtles and large fish, but are usually only a danger to goslings. Don Payne, who fed and observed the geese for fourteen years, told me he has seen many goslings pulled under by snappers in Silver Lake. Don also related an incredible story. A snapper grabbed an adult goose by the foot. The goose flapped around, and after much effort, escaped, perhaps minus part of its foot.

Of course, the ultimate danger the geese have had to cope with has been human. A prized game bird, geese have had many decades to develop skills needed to foil hunters. Yet, the same birds that are extremely wary when hunted are quick to recognize where they are protected, and may even take feed from a person's hand in the city park.

This behavior leads to not very common, but often comical, attempts at "goosenapping." Tony Stegen and Jack Heather, of the Minnesota Department of Natural Resources, recounted the following incidents at

Should an eagle fly over, all the geese fall silent and swim to the center of the lake.

The Triumph Ceremony is displayed between related geese such as siblings.

Silver Lake.

Tony saw a man with a stick in his hand hiding behind a tree. At the end of the stick was a noose laid out on the ground. His partner was spreading corn, attempting to lure in a goose. When Tony asked the man just what he was up to, the man, apparently concentrating so hard at his task that he was unaware he was talking to a game official, explained that he was waiting for a goose to step in the noose so he could catch it.

Jack commented that many neighborhood eyes watch out for the flock, then told about a goose that fended quite well for itself. He had been watching some teenagers feeding geese near a van with its side door open. One youth grabbed a goose by the neck and flung it into the van, shutting the door behind it. Jack had started towards the van when suddenly the door opened wide and out flew the goose. In its fright, it had pretty well sprayed the entire interior of the van. Imagine the panic inside the van as they hurried to open the door!

If the morning is warm, the geese are quick to begin their day, but following cold nights, when their feathers are flocked with rime, they may sleep quite late.

Geese often bathe and preen soon after awakening. Spreading their wings slightly and dipping their heads into the water, they toss water over their backs. Occasionally, extra exuberance is put into the bath. The birds dive frenetically under water or tumble forward in the water, feet kicking the air, then roll onto their sides and vigorously beat the water with their wings. This wild activity seems contagious and may spread through the whole flock. Although the geese sometimes preen on water, they more often stand in the shallows near shore. Rubbing their heads over the preen glands at the bases of their tails, they spread the oil to all their feathers. Meticulous grooming with the bill keeps the feathers' tiny connecting barbs intact.

After preening, the geese may begin milling about, with each family winding its way single file among the mass of geese covering the lake. Presently, the flock grows restless, and gander after gander swims with head high, neck forward, and chin up, shaking his head, trumpeting excitedly. Soon the morning feeding flights begin. Each gander's calls are echoed by his family and reach a crescendo as the birds run over

During cold nights, the geese become covered with a thick layer of frost.

16

Bathing is often the first activity of the day. Typically, the head is dipped into the lake and water tossed over the back.

Following bathing the geese usually return to shore to preen their feathers.

Although capable of near vertical take-offs, geese usually run over the water until flight speed is achieved.

the water gaining the speed needed for flight.

The build-up of all of this head shaking serves to synchronize the members of the family; other geese, watching, are warned of impending takeoffs—a system that works well, but is not foolproof. I was watching the morning exodus from a narrow stretch of the lake when a family rose up in front of another group that had just taken to the air. One of the geese was struck from behind and tumbled back into the water.

It may take more than an hour for the flights to nearly empty the lake. Flying around forty miles per hour at an altitude of one hundred to one thousand feet, the geese may disperse twenty or more miles to fields they will feed in that day.

Historically these geese fed on prairie grasses, turning their heads sideways to strip seeds from the stems. Now they glean waste kernels from rows of corn stubble. As the flock feeds, some geese remain alert sentries. Feeding in a large flock means each goose can spend more time feeding and less time watching for danger. Should a threat appear, the flock rises up in a wave—a dark blanket covers the sky, and the honking cries of alarm are not heard individually, but as a vibrating hum, like an enormous swarm of bees. The geese assess the danger and may soon settle down in the field, some distance from the site of the danger.

When done feeding, the geese return to Silver Lake as they came, lifting off as families, often combining with other families to form Vs for the flight home, especially if they were feeding in a distant location.

As the geese near the lake, they begin a long descending glide; wings are set, bodies held upright with necks arched and heads high. Each bird's posture is identical to all the others' as the formation floats down over the treetops. Then the show begins—out of almost every arriving flock, several birds suddenly sideslip, quickly losing altitude. Some do a half barrel-roll, turning completely onto their backs while keeping their heads upright. The daredevil maneuvers last but a split second, then the birds regain a smooth, orderly glide, turn into the wind, and with feet out and tail down, slide into the water. There is much vocalizing between the incoming birds and those on the lake, and among regrouping families once they have landed.

The afternoon is spent swimming, preening, and sleeping. The tamer

Traditionally geese fed on prairie grasses. Now their primary winter food is corn.

geese take advantage of handouts of corn from park visitors. Occasionally squabbles break out, usually followed by the loud brassy Triumph Ceremony.

On most days, the geese make a second feeding flight late in the afternoon, returning to the lake around sunset.

As the snow melts away in March, the geese feed more on the tender new shoots of green grasses, and less in the corn fields. The grasses are rich in protein, and in the month preceding spring migration, the geese put on considerable weight. The added weight is needed to fuel the upcoming migration north to breeding grounds, and to sustain the geese through the nesting season, during which they eat very little until the goslings are hatched.

Pair bonding takes place among some yearling geese, who are too young to breed, on their summer range. By the end of their second winter at Silver Lake, most geese have secured a mate. The courting seems to be initiated by the gander, with the female choosing from among her suitors. Tony Stegen observed a neck-collared gander swimming beside a goose with his neck fully extended, obviously trying to gain her favor, for most of a winter afternoon. Several days later, the same neck-collared gander was seen alone. The female had apparently rejected him. With the approach of spring, ganders become more aggressive in their attempts to win and defend mates; and threats, chases, and fights occur frequently.

I watched a particularly protracted fight take place on new ice. The two ganders gripped each other's breasts with their bills and repeatedly struck violent blows with their wings. After several minutes, one bird obviously admitted defeat. The victor, however, refused to release his hold. With a wrenching turn, the loser tore away, but was immediately grabbed again by the tail as he was making his escape. Calling in distress, he attempted a takeoff, but no matter how fast he spun his feet or how hard he flapped his wings, all he could manage was to drag his backpeddling adversary about thirty feet over the slick ice. At that point, the exhausted bird simply collapsed on the ice, wings spread, head and neck flat out before him. Feeling now completely the winner, the other gander let go and returned to his mate, or potential mate, for whom he put on a lengthy Triumph Ceremony.

Once formed, pair bonds remain intact as long as both birds are together. If they become separated, or one is killed, the other takes a new mate. During the spring migration, the gander travels with his mate as she leads him to the nesting ground where she was born. (Captive-raised females that have been released are believed to return to the location of their first flight.) Most two-year-old geese establish nesting territories, but many will not breed and nest until the following year.

Some copulation occurs prior to spring migration. The sequence shown in the photographs took place on March 20 at Silver Lake. To begin, both birds dipped their heads into the water and threw it over their backs as in bathing, only with the wings closed. This activity went on, increasing in intensity, for a few minutes. Gradually the gander swam closer to the goose and laid his neck over her back several times. Finally he swam behind her and mounted, grasping the back of her neck with his bill. The copulation was over in a matter of seconds, during which the goose was completely submerged. Once he was off her, they faced each other, and both birds stretched their necks up and back, tilting their bills into the air. The gander lifted his wings slightly in a swan-like pose and emitted a brief, quiet murmur. The goose raised up, flapping her wings. Then they both resumed the water tossing ritual, and vigorously preened for several minutes, rubbing the tops of their heads over their backs.

A few of the geese nest at Silver Lake and in the surrounding areas, but most depart northward. The geese reach the nesting area in Manitoba between March 20 and April 12, three to six days after leaving Silver Lake. Giant Canada geese nest earlier than any other waterfowl, and the marshes are usually still frozen when they arrive.

Once at the nesting ground, the yearlings, and other nonbreeding birds, continue on a secondary migration that takes them high into the Arctic to the Thelon River region, where they feed on the nutritious arctic plants. Following the molt and regrowth of primary flight feathers, they will rejoin the flock at the nesting grounds.

Meanwhile, the mated pairs attempt to establish territories in which to nest. The ideal territory is close to water and feeding areas. The geese need emergent vegetation to take cover in during the molt and prefer an isolated nesting site with an open view of the surroundings.

The mating ritual of Canada geese begins with both geese tossing water over their backs. Gradually the gander approaches the goose and eventually mounts her, grasping the back of her neck during the brief copulation. The gander then raises his wings slightly and with head tilted up gives a muted call. After a few moments of this posturing, both birds resume the water tossing, and finally preen themselves.

THELON RIVER AREA

INTERLAKE REGION

MARSHY POINT

DELTA WINNIPEG

MINNEAPOLIS/ST. PAUL

SILVER LAKE

Most of the geese from Silver Lake nest in the Interlake Region between Lake Winnipegosis, Lake Manitoba, and Lake Winnipeg. Many of the non-nesting birds make a secondary migration to the Thelon River Area.

The pairs may have to put up an intense fight to win a territory. Once acquired, aggressive vocalizations and displays usually suffice to defend it, although brief fighting occurs throughout the nesting period. While both birds protect the territory, the male is more aggressive.

Within two weeks after the pair establish their territory, the female makes the nest and begins laying. A typical nest is a hollowed depression on top of a muskrat house, although a wide variety of sites may be used, including predator-proof nesting platforms built by conservationists. The goose gathers surrounding vegetation for the nest, forming a rim from one and a half to four feet across with an inside diameter of about ten inches. After laying three or four eggs, the female plucks her breast to add down to the nest.

The average clutch size of creamy white eggs is a little over five, laid at a rate of about one every day and a half.

The goose incubates the eggs for about twenty-eight days. During this time, the gander stands guard nearby and accompanies the goose in the morning and late afternoon when she takes short breaks to drink, feed, and preen. He is a fearless guardian, and stories abound of ganders attacking people while protecting their mates and nests. I made the mistake of wading between a goose and gander in the spring of 1970, and received the gander's wrath on my back as I splashed to shore.

About seventy percent of the nests have eggs that hatch, with predation and desertion being the leading causes of failure.

About a day after the young hatch, the goose leads them to feeding areas. The gander brings up the rear of the line. He now defends whatever area the family travels through, just as he protected the nesting area. The young birds feed some on aquatic insects and invertebrates, but they obtain the bulk of their food by grazing on vegetation. At night, and during inclement weather, the goose broods her goslings, providing warmth and protection.

When the young are three or four weeks old, the parent birds begin to molt. They are flightless for about a month, while the new feathers are growing in. Both the adults and young start flying about the same time.

The territorial aggressiveness that was so evident early in the spring

The average number in a clutch of eggs is a little over five.

The goose incubates her eggs for about twenty-eight days, turning the eggs often.

26

Goslings are brooded most of their first day of life. They venture out on wobbly legs to explore the area around the nest, then return to the warmth and security beneath the goose. This clutch hatched out during the evening and night. By 4:00 P.M., twenty-four hours after the first egg began to crack, they were taking their first brief swim.

29

is now largely gone, and the families flock and feed together, now joined by the nonbreeding birds that have returned from their secondary migration.

The giants were the first of the Canada geese to migrate north in the spring, and they are the last to leave for the south. The first migrating geese reach Silver Lake the third week of September; the bulk of the flock arrives between the last week of October and the third week of November.

The young geese experience their first, and most perilous, hunting season. Most of the Silver Lake geese that are shot are taken while they are still on the breeding grounds in Manitoba. The Minnesota season generally runs from the beginning of October into the fourth week of December, with a week off in mid-December. In the years 1976 through 1986, an average of 1,588 geese a year were downed by hunters in the Rochester area. About a quarter of those were not retrievable, largely due to inexperienced hunters mistaking the range of the big birds. Many geese have feathers broken by pellets, and by the time they are adults, over half the geese will carry shot.

The population of the flock is closely monitored, and hunting helps to keep the birds' numbers within the carrying capacity of the area, benefiting the overall health of the flock.

The number of geese at Silver Lake peaks around the third week in November. From then through the first week in January, the flock gradually diminishes as some geese move further south. Many of the departing birds end up in either Crab Orchard National Wildlife Refuge in Illinois or Swan Lake National Wildlife Refuge in Missouri. The geese left at Silver Lake in mid-January are likely to stay the rest of the winter.

Now that so many geese have come to depend on Silver Lake, what would happen if the power plant—Silver Lake's source of open water— were to close? I put the question to Joe Hensel of the Rochester Public Utilities. The power plant probably will be operating into the twenty-first century, and in the meantime, alternative means of keeping the water open are being discussed. So, the annual spectacle of thousands of Canada geese filling the lake in the city park seems to be one we will be able to share with coming generations.

Many geese that are wounded by hunters later die at Silver Lake.

"I could hear the geese high overhead, the glorious gabbling only they can achieve, a sound that seems to hold all the wild freedom of the wilderness, of continental expanses, of the unseen and unknown of far places."

SIGURD F. OLSON
The Hidden Forest

"A warm cloudy, rain-threatening morning . . . The sonorous, quavering sounds of the geese are the voice of this cloudy air,—a sound that comes from directly between us and the sky; an aerial sound, and yet so distinct, heavy, and sonorous a clanking chain drawn through the heavy air."

HENRY DAVID THOREAU, 1857

"They carry weight, such a weight of metal in the air. Their dark waved outline as they disappear. The grenadiers of the air. Man pigmifies himself at sight of these inhabitants of the air."

HENRY DAVID THOREAU, 1852

"I can imagine before me one who has just accomplished the defeat of another male after a struggle of half an hour or more. He advances gallantly toward the object of contention, his head scarcely raised an inch from the ground, his bill open to its full stretch, his fleshy tongue elevated, his eyes darting fiery glances, and as he moves he hisses loudly, while the emotion which he experiences causes his quills to shake and his feathers to rustle. Now he is close to her who in his eyes is all loveliness; his neck bending gracefully in all directions, passes all round her, and occasionally touches her body; and as she congratulates him on his victory, and acknowledges his affection, they move their necks in a hundred curious ways."

JOHN JAMES AUDUBON, 1840

"*Canadas came down in open water ahead of us, and I was amazed again at the buoyant way they had of alighting. It seemed to me the great geese came down so much more easily than any of the ducks did, a strange thing for these heavier birds.*"

FLORENCE PAGE JAQUES
The Geese Fly High

"*They seemed to me the most enormous birds I had ever seen, fabulous creatures, as they loomed above our flimsy shelter . . . We were breathless each time they passed, their powerful slow beating wings blocking off the foggy light above us.*"

FLORENCE PAGE JAQUES
The Geese Fly High

"You first hear a faint honking from one or two in the northeast and think there are but a few wandering there, but, looking up, see forty or fifty coming in a more or less broken harrow, wedging their way southwest."

HENRY DAVID THOREAU, 1857

"Were the weapons more deadly, feats of chivalry would now be performed; as it is, thrust and blow succeed each other like the strokes of hammers driven by sturdy forger. But now, the mated gander has caught hold of his antagonist's head with his bill; no bulldog can cling faster to his victim; he squeezes him with all the energy of rage, lashes him with powerful wings, and at length drives him away, spreads out his pinions, runs with joy to his mate, and fills the air with cries of exultation."

JOHN JAMES AUDUBON, 1840

". . . at length the leaders summon their hosts to meet on high; and forming in two long converg-*
ing lines, pointing toward the already feeble rays of the noonday sun, they start. High in the air
they travel on, cheered by the clarion call of the leader, answered at frequent intervals by his followers,
far above all dangers and straight along the well-known path."

ARTHUR CLEVELAND BENT
Life Histories of North American Wild Fowl

REFERENCES

Bellrose, Frank C. *Ducks, Geese, and Swans of North America*. 2d ed. revised. Harrisburg, Penn.: Stackpole Books, 1978.

Bent, Arthur C. *Life Histories of North American Waterfowl*. Smithsonian Institution United States Bulletin 130, 1925. Reprint. New York: Dover Publications, 1962.

Burton, Robert. *Bird Behavior*. New York: Alfred A. Knopf, 1985.

Cooper, J. A. "The History and Nesting Biology of Canada Geese at Marshy Point, Manitoba." Ph.D. diss., University of Massachusetts, Amherst, 1973.

Cruickshank, Helen. *Thoreau On Birds*. New York: McGraw-Hill Book Company, 1964.

Davis, Tom. "Giants In The Sky." *Sporting Classics* (Nov./Dec. 1988): 42–52.

Delacour, Jean. *The Waterfowl of the World*. Vol. 1. London: Country Life; New York: Arco Publishing Company, Inc., 1954.

Gulden, Nicholas A., and Leon L. Johnson. "History, Behavior and Management of a Flock of Giant Canada Geese in Southeastern Minnesota." In *Canada Goose Management: Current Continental Problems and Programs*, edited by Ruth L. Hine and Clay Schoenfeld. Madison, Wis.: Dumbar Educational Services, 1968.

Hanson, Harold C. *The Giant Canada Goose*. Carbondale and Edwardsville: Southern Illinois University Press, 1965.

Hochbaum, Albert H. *Travels and Traditions of Waterfowl*. Minneapolis: University of Minnesota Press, 1955.

Jacques, Florence P. *The Geese Fly High*. Minneapolis: University of Minnesota Press, 1939.

Johnsgard, Paul A. *Water Fowl, Their Biology and Natural History*. Lincoln: University of Nebraska Press, 1968.

McLandress, Murray R. "Behavioral and Physiological Changes of Giant Canada Geese (*Branta canadensis maxima*) Prior to Spring Migration." M.S. thesis, University of California, Davis, 1979.

North Dakota Game & Fish Department. *Rearing and Restoring Giant Canada Geese in the Dakotas*. Bismark, 1984.

Savage, Candace Sherk. *Wings of the North: A Gallery of Favorite Birds*. Minneapolis: University of Minnesota Press, 1985 (Published in Canada by Western Producer Prairie Books as *The Wonder of Canadian Birds*).

Terres, John K. *The Audubon Society Encyclopedia of North American Birds*. New York: Alfred A. Knopf, 1980.

Wechsler, Charles A. "Winged Giants of Silver Lake." *Minnesota Volunteer* 42 (Jan./Feb. 1979): 54–64.

Wetmore, Alexander. *Water, Prey, and Game Birds of North America*. Washington, D.C.: National Geographic Society, 1965.

Windish, Leo. *Wings of Autumn*. (Available at the Rochester Public Library in Minnesota).